SUBMARINES

Valerie Bodden

CREATIVE ✦ EDUCATION

Published by Creative Education
P.O. Box 227, Mankato, Minnesota 56002
Creative Education is an imprint of The Creative Company
www.thecreativecompany.us

Design and production by Liddy Walseth
Art direction by Rita Marshall
Printed by Corporate Graphics in the United States of America

Photographs by DefenseImagery (MC1 James Kimber), Getty Images (Check Six, Bill Curtsinger,
Keystone, Haywood Magee/Picture Post, J. Baylor Roberts/National Geographic, SuperStock,
Adam K. Thomas/U.S. Navy, Sam Yeh/AFP), iStockphoto (James Dare, Geoffrey Holman, Naphtalina),
Shutterstock (Ensuper, Ranga Yogeshwalka)

Library of Congress Cataloging-in-Publication Data

Bodden, Valerie.
Submarines / by Valerie Bodden.
p. cm. — (Built for battle)
Includes bibliographical references and index.
Summary: A fundamental exploration of submarines, including their size and diving ability, history of
development, periscopes and other features, and famous models from around the world.
ISBN 978-1-60818-128-5
1. Submarines (Ships)—Juvenile literature. I. Title.
VM365.B59 2012
623.825'7—dc22   2010054405

CPSIA: 070212 PO1591

2 4 6 8 9 7 5 3

BUILT for BATTLE

SUBMARINES

Valerie Bodden

TABLE OF

contents

A huge boat moves quietly through the water.

But no one sees it. It is far below the waves.

Suddenly, it fires a TORPEDO at an enemy ship.

This is a submarine!

A submarine is a boat that can move both under the water and on top of it. It attacks enemy ships and submarines. Most submarines travel through the water at 20 to 40 miles (32-64 km) per hour.

A rocket blasting off

from an American

submarine in the 1950s

A submarine called the *Nautilus* was the first to use nuclear power

The first military submarines were built more than 200 years ago. They had room for only one person! The person had to turn a crank to make the submarine move. Later, submarines were made much bigger. People added ENGINES. In the 1950s, some submarines began to run on NUCLEAR POWER.

Famous Submarine ★
Type VIIC U-Boat

COUNTRY

Germany

ENTERED SERVICE

1940

LENGTH

220 feet (67.1 m)

WIDTH

20 feet (6.1 m)

WEIGHT

975 tons (884 t)

FASTEST SPEED

20 miles (32 km) per hour

CREW

44

Germany built more than 500 Type VIIC U-boats during WORLD WAR II. They were not as big as other submarines of the 1940s, but they sank many enemy ships.

A submarine's body is long and rounded. The smallest submarines are only about 150 feet (45.7 m) long. The longest submarines are more than 550 feet (168 m) long. That is as long as one and a half football fields! Submarines can be from 15 to 75 feet (4.6-22.9 m) wide.

Inside, a submarine has eating and sleeping areas. It has a control room, too. The control room has everything crew members need to steer the submarine and fire its weapons.

The control room of this submarine is lit up with red lights

Submarines do not have windows. Instead, they have periscopes. Periscopes are long tubes that a person can look through to see what is happening above the water. The newest submarines use cameras on posts instead of periscopes.

Typhoon Class

COUNTRY

Soviet Union/Russia

ENTERED SERVICE

1981

LENGTH

574 feet (175 m)

WIDTH

76 feet (23.2 m)

WEIGHT

48,000 tons (43,545 t)

FASTEST SPEED

31 miles (50 km) per hour

CREW

150

Typhoon class submarines are the biggest submarines in the world! Even though they are so big, they are very quiet and can turn easily.

A commanding officer is in charge of a submarine.

Most submarines have 25 to 150 crew members.

The crew members live in the tight space of the

submarine for months at a time.

A submarine traveling

with an aircraft carrier

and other ships

During a war, a submarine might travel ahead of or behind other warships. It can protect the warships from enemies. Submarines can fire torpedoes or MISSILES (*MIS-sulz*) at enemy ships. They can launch missiles toward targets on land, too.

Virginia Class

COUNTRY

United States

ENTERED SERVICE

2004

LENGTH

377 feet (115 m)

WIDTH

34 feet (10.4 m)

WEIGHT

7,800 tons (7,076 t)

FASTEST SPEED

28 miles (45 km) per hour

CREW

134

Virginia class submarines can dive in the shallow water near shore. Or they can dive more than 800 feet (244 m) under the water. These submarines have cameras instead of periscopes.

A submarine rising

to the surface after a

long dive underwater

To escape enemies, submarines dive deep.
They move fast. That way, they stay safe to
fight another day!

GLOSSARY

engines—machines that use energy to make things, such as cars or submarines, move

missiles—exploding weapons that are pushed through the air by rockets to hit a target

nuclear power—a type of energy created when tiny parts of certain kinds of metals split apart

torpedo—an underwater weapon like a missile that pushes itself through the water to hit a target and explode

World War II—a war from 1939 to 1945 in which the U.S., Great Britain, France, and the Soviet Union fought against Germany, Italy, and Japan

INDEX

WEB SITES

NOVA Online: Submarines, Secrets, and Spies

http://www.pbs.org/wgbh/nova/subsecrets/spriconhi.html

Explore a map and pictures of the inside of a submarine.

Super Coloring: Military Coloring Pages

http://www.supercoloring.com/pages/category/military/

Print and color pictures of all your favorite military machines.

READ MORE

Demarest, Chris. *Alpha, Bravo, Charlie: The Military Alphabet*. New York: Margaret K. McElderry Books, 2005.

Mitton, Tony. *Super Submarines*. Boston: Kingfisher, 2006.